THE
INNKEEPER'S STORY

THE
INNKEEPER'S STORY

STEVE KNIGHTON & SHANE KNIGHTON

XULON PRESS

Xulon Press
2301 Lucien Way #415
Maitland, FL 32751
407.339.4217
www.xulonpress.com

© 2023 by Steve Knighton & Shane Knighton

All rights reserved solely by the author. The author guarantees all contents are original and do not infringe upon the legal rights of any other person or work. No part of this book may be reproduced in any form without the permission of the author.

Due to the changing nature of the Internet, if there are any web addresses, links, or URLs included in this manuscript, these may have been altered and may no longer be accessible. The views and opinions shared in this book belong solely to the author and do not necessarily reflect those of the publisher. The publisher therefore disclaims responsibility for the views or opinions expressed within the work.

Unless otherwise indicated, Scripture quotations taken from the Holy Bible, New International Version (NIV). Copyright © 1973, 1978, 1984, 2011 by Biblica, Inc.™. Used by permission. All rights reserved.

Paperback ISBN-13: 978-1-66287-123-8
Ebook ISBN-13: 978-1-66287-124-5

Acknowledgements

I am most grateful to my son Shane for entertaining the notion that we might collaborate and complete this short story. He gently pressured me to attempt this joint adventure. I'm forever appreciative to have had this opportunity. Shane has always been a risk taker. Well, there was that one time we opted out of the bungie jump in Colorado. His life has not always been easy but God's grace is sufficient and God's strength is made great in our weakness.

My wife Kathy has always been my biggest cheerleader and throughout the months of working on this issue she has constantly encouraged and applauded the work in progress. Her daily devotionals culminate in her fervent praying for family, friends and the future of the faithful. And by extension this story. She is a blessing to so many, but especially me. She has a servant's heart.

A shout out to my sister-in-law, Betty Ann Knighton, for the painstaking effort she put into editing the rough draft. As a religion major and a former high school English teacher she provided an unparalleled perspective and polish to the story.

A special thank you to Reverend David Stroud, M.D., my brother-in-law; my brother, David Knighton, Sharon Brooks and Carolyn Saul for reading the rough drafts and adding their suggestions to make it a better work. And to the Valentines and golf buddies for their weekly encouragement.

Lastly to my granddaughter Abigail for the illustration. She is an amazing young lady.

INTRODUCTION
THE INNKEEPER'S STORY

My father and mother were both Christians from a very early age. As an adult Dad served, at least once, on every board and committee church bureaucracies deem necessary. Mother was the church organist for at least fifty years before crippling arthritis robbed her of this ministry. Their six children, I was the second, were dutifully reared in the biblical interpretations and subsequent teachings of Baptists.

Growing up in a church provided me with many opportunities to hear the famous Gospel stories over and over as the liturgical seasons unfolded. Some passages would often oblige further explanation that I felt was necessary to satisfy my obsessive-compulsive nature. For instance, how did Jesus get from the cross to the tomb? Or who owned the colt Jesus rode into Jerusalem? Those personally necessary clarifications were lacking scriptural reference and the local pastors could offer little more than perhaps that it wasn't essential to the more salient spiritual point. I disagreed.

The Innkeeper's Story

Upon becoming a father, I determined that my children would also be provided the spiritual nurturing offered by the church and to that end dutifully made certain we were in regular attendance.

When my son Shane, a retired USAF Lt. Colonel with a Ph.D., asked me to coauthor this short story, I was surprised, but welcomed the challenge and the collaboration.

The Innkeeper's Story is a work of much fiction that is an intriguing supposition. Suppose I could posit more details in the birth of Jesus to make it more viable. Who delivered the baby? We tell you! Who was the man that owned the colt Jesus rode into Jerusalem? We will share that too. And how did Jesus' body get from the cross to the tomb? Yes. We will share a prospect.

We trust you will enjoy this didactic short story and that your OCD will be lessened by these plausible but unproven possibilities.

THE INNKEEPER'S STORY

My wife Bina and I built this little inn three years ago when we first got married. I wanted so much more for her than I've been able to provide. Our little inn has five rooms to let, on the upwind side of the road from Jericho up to Jerusalem near the city of Motza. Being upwind is a small

The Innkeeper's Story

blessing, the road is a rough thoroughfare and not for the faint of heart or those queasy to noxious odors. Bandits, Gentiles, and Samaritans gallivant up and down the road and cause all kind of mischief as those of that kind tend to do. I want to take Bina away from this town, off this dangerous road, and maybe into Jerusalem.

CHAPTER ONE
THE SAMARITAN ENIGMA

Upon answering the inferiorly crafted wooden door I was fully intending to forcefully admonish the sojourner that, although I needed his commerce, I was none too happy with the incessant and continual clamor against the insufficient entryway. As the echoing door was yanked open, I was grateful that my disparaging word choice got caught in my throat. He was conspicuously dressed, was of a natural ruddy complexion and could have easily passed as any other traveling Jew had it not been for the obviously absent talliths. Those tassels that were required as a way of identifying a Jew. 1. (Numbers 15:37-41)

My eyes were irrationally relocated from his money belt to the bloody bundle atop his animal. That man was not just any unfortunate, but a Jew. My scarcity of breath was attributed to thoughts of this becoming my abrupt fate also. Any Samaritan brazen enough to attack a son of Abraham would have no hesitation in doling out comparable offense to a trifling innkeeper.

The Innkeeper's Story

    I awaited my destiny with no consideration for the subsequent conversation.

    Apparently, my impatient traveler happened upon the aforementioned brutally beaten Semitic a league or two down the route and had taken mercy to an extreme. He was now suggesting that I, another avowed by tradition hater of Samaritans everywhere, provide refuge for the incapacitated Jewish brethren. And that he, one despised by all godly men in Judah, would compensate me for this compassionate effort. He produced legitimate coinage to solidify his commitment, even offering to provide more currency should more be required on his return trip. I was still suspicious of this entreaty. Perhaps greed or apprehension motivated me to accept, but I agreed and assisted my newly acquired Samaritan friend in gingerly removing this half-conscious victim to my humble couch. The two other boarders would be relegated to the straw mattresses in the opposite corner. Perhaps a small refund to them.

    Days later as I mulled over this incredulous encounter, I kept recollecting my prejudicial religious upbringing and how I was tainted to despise the neighbors in our community that confessed to having 'Samaritan' as a legacy. Why again did we hate them? Oh yeah, they married outside our faith. Not purists. Our flaunted supremacy was violated while we were in exile for ignoring our worship of God.

    This heretofore loathsome Samaritan 2 (2Kings 17:27-33) had become an enigma to me. I pondered the motives he must have had for effectively saving this stranger's life.

Was he going to run for office and wanted to boast of community activism? Did he have little regard for political correctness? Was he just being a holier than thou chest beater type.

Hard to know I suppose. But what was undeniable was his compassion and tangible response. Was he a better man than I? I can't imagine myself reacting in a similar manner were the roles reversed. Touching the Samaritan would have been a stretch. But to take my precious time to pick him up and lead him to safety was beyond logic. Let alone the benevolence of paying someone to care for him.

Weren't Samaritans a lesser people? How was it that I was secretly admiring this man? I need to shake off this compelling sense of respect and revert to my preconceived and pernicious paranoia of pagans.

Still.......... this pagan was modeling a behavior that was ostensibly the most important. Love!!

Didn't I read in Leviticus 19:34 "The stranger who resides with you shall be to you as the native among you; and you shall love him as yourself. For you were aliens in the land of Egypt: I am the Lord your God"? Do you suppose this was the teaching that inclined our mystery man to manifest mercy to a broken brother of Israel? After all they do believe in the Torah.

Too many questions. Not enough guidance. I will ask at the synagogue.

I am intrigued and confused by this act of grace. It has challenged my doctrine and raised my bar of human

The Innkeeper's Story

kindness that I have set purposefully low. Dealing with drifters is inherently tedious, and trustworthiness is not a trait I inherited.

CHAPTER TWO
THE BETHLEHEM BYWAY

I have convinced Bina that our future isn't in this ostensibly unsafe town. I need to make arrangements for pulling our meager cartful of possessions to the suburbs of Jerusalem. Less taxation outside the city gates and foot traffic there is a constant as pilgrims and traders enter the Holy City.

While skeptical of this sudden departure she agreed to the relocation. I am fairly certain she has noticed the perceptible angst I am showing whenever our inn door is loudly rapped upon by potential customers. The episode involving a bloody boarder and his benefactor has left a fearful impression on us residing in the immediate neighborhood. This latest wayside mugging and why the Samaritan would instruct me to attend to his wounds and provide payment for said palliative care has made me wary and perplexed.

It would be years before I learned our Messiah would recount this distinguishable occasion and ascribe His own adjective to this Samaritan – Good. 3.(Luke 10: 30-35)

This would ultimately identify this individual forever and continually conjure the instructive commandment of Jesus. Love thy neighbor as thyself. Ostensibly a virtue not yet accepted among the masses.

I consider myself a competent carpenter and decide to lighten the burden upon my beast by selling used, but still sturdy, furniture. I will need to modernize my new inn anyway and am thinking of a universal décor for all rooms. We celebrate many holidays as a culture – Pesach (Passover, Shavuot (Pentecost), and Sukkot (Tabernacles), when the Israelites of Judah would travel to the Holy City of Jerusalem. Possibly I could commission sketches that reflect each holiday and proudly display them on our porch. I conceive of becoming a holiday stop. A welcoming holiday inn to weary travelers. My reach is exceeding my grasp.

Anyway, my mind is still filled with the mystery of the correlation of events recently thrust upon me. A merciful Samaritan, the appearance of a wary rabbi and the sudden urge to abandon the status quo for a more promising livelihood. I needed clarification. An explanation that would quell this uneasiness eroding my Shalom.

And this Samaritan! He was an enigma. His actions violated every scintilla of historic nurture. We were deliberately taught as youth this discrimination of ethnicity. Samaritans were considered an impure, disgraced, and a pathetic people. But this Samaritan. He was a paradox.

I felt compelled to admit admiration and respect for his actions. And when Jesus elevated this story to perpetuity

The Innkeeper's Story

by His teachings, my esteem for the Good Samaritan was vindicated.

I travel on toward my destiny in the small burb of Bethlehem, content to leave the shechem (ridge). Not yet knowing that God's grand plan for incarnation would include a pitiful innkeeper. An innkeeper deeply affected by the morality modeled by a man of accidental acquaintance. Again, with these Good Samaritan ethics! They are unsettling!

I have chosen Bethlehem to invigorate my family and finances. Its proximity to Jerusalem leads me to imagine a steady stream of pilgrims who will need room and board. And it just so happens I provide both, for a shekel. Per person over the age of twelve. Per night.

After viewing parcels available for purchase, I conclude a transaction that includes a modest fixer upper made of limestone blocks. Three small rooms currently but with ample room for expansion. The thatch is in need of repair, but I use this as leverage to gain a more than fair reduction in the asking price.

This limestone is found on my purchased acreage. Caves have already been expanded as this rock is excavated for buildings. Limestone is used for a structure intended to last for generations. My children's children will benefit from my shrewd bartering. And with the continual excavation, the caves are becoming more and more suitable as the natural enclosure for my livestock.

The Innkeeper's Story

I envision the need to acquire a few sheep, a cow, some chickens and of course a place for my trusty steed, the mule. These should provide for the guests and by extension – me. Thusly I'll need a convenient and safe quarters for them. This hollowed out limestone stable should suffice.

CHAPTER THREE
THE LITTLE DRUMMER BOY

The prickly vegetation is abundant among the craggy slopes that comprise my property. The sheep and goats appear to be less discerning about their diet than most animals and eagerly devour this undergrowth. As an innkeeper I had relied almost exclusively on the local grain merchant to supply me with edibles for my small menagerie. Now that I am expanding my business interests, I will be enlarging the creatures necessary for supporting the B, breakfast, in B & B.

I have befriended young Seth, a hardy, local shepherd boy, and will hopefully access his acumen when it comes to finding the livestock. I may even hire him to manage this segment of my enterprise. The segment having to do with excrement removal and outside slopping was not deemed a part of my managerial duties I declared.

Like many shepherds of his tender age, Seth has developed skills in defense of his flock. He possesses an accurate aim and is quite accomplished with his crude but effective sling shot. I have personally seen him down an energetic quail to provide a tasty bird for his family's dinner. His crude staff, probably just an aptly shaped branch detached from a fig tree, was skillfully used to return a wandering lamb to the fold.

And although formidable in the protection of his charges, Seth also enjoys the talent of drumming those same sheep into a quiet submission of security. His strong, lithe fingers move effortlessly across the leather of his daraba (drum). The tones emanated are melodic and soothing and resonate for some distance. It's little wonder his sheep stay calm and close as he plays.

In ancient times certain drums were made from a clay jar, with a donkey skin stretched over the big open side. Some drums were made of wood with leather stretched over the open end. Many Torah accounts included the joy derived from the instruments of our ancestors. King David was said to have danced in praise to God.

Yes, the lad was special. I would posit a very special future. After all, didn't God require the prophet Samuel to anoint another special shepherd boy as the imminent King of Israel? King David! 4. (1Samuel 16:1) Why couldn't this smelly and lower caste shepherd boy pull himself up by his sandal thongs? I've certainly witnessed stranger occurrences of late. Who could comprehend the shunned Samaritan's merciful and costly act? Not I. I've already wasted an inordinate amount of time dwelling on the irrational.

The Innkeeper's Story

My new boarding house was quickly becoming a reality. I had secured the site, hired contractors to expand the limestone rooms, acquired chickens, livestock and sheep, interviewed support staff and was constructing new furniture. I was moving in the fast lane. Came to recall there was actually only a single, rocky and rough lane and that that comparison was humbling and more accurate.

I was delighted to have had the extra currency that had providentially been attained via the Good Samaritan to partiality fund my venture here in Bethlehem. God is good and provides. Strange how the encounter with that Samaritan has impacted my perspective, my pension and my prospectus. I am constantly retelling this adventure to my transient boarders. Most aren't amused. The Jews they shrug and grumble nearly inaudible expletives about conspiracy motives for helping the wounded brother. The foreign guests barely understand the significance.

I find it compelling.

CHAPTER FOUR
EMPERORS, KINGS AND PRIESTS

We have just gotten word that a decree went out from Emperor Augustus that all the world should be registered. 5.(Luke 2:1-4) Registered is a euphemism for 'everybody' pay up. Do the kings of this earth collect taxes from their own people or just from foreigners? Judging from the percentage they ascribe as my just due, I'm inclined to believe I pay for the lavish trappings of Roman power here all by myself. The only silver lining is that many more wayfarers will be needing lodging as they are forced from all over Israel to come to Bethlehem. King David was a native Bethlemite. Bethlemian. Bethlemonian. Anyway, he grew up around here, and all of his lineage will necessarily be required to register and will need an inn. I step in to fill this essential need. It should be noted that King David was rather a progressive monarch and his progeny are extreme. Supply and demand for those claiming a bloodline to King David will undoubtedly cause my nightly room rates to increase as they descend upon this tiny hamlet to register.

Any reasonable and astute Jew knows that paying taxes can be for the glory of God. Wasn't it Moses on direction of God that instructed the Israelites to pay a ransom for his life and thereby avoid a plague? 6.(Exodus 30:11-16) This tax was then to be used to restore the Tent of Meeting and be an individual sacrifice given to God. And again, when King Joash required all from Judah and the assembly of Israel to be taxed to repair the Temple? They all gave eagerly and beyond as they were blessed.

But this Roman taxation was burdensome and pagan and additional to Herod's. No one is eager to comply. Our kinsmen that are enlisted to complete this Roman sanctioned burglary are vilified and despised. Albeit they are under orders to perform this onerous task while we self-righteous businessmen feel far less guilt raising goods and rents to deepen our profit. A distinction without a difference?

I worship at the Temple in Jerusalem from time to time. I can rationalize compelling reasons for not attending every Sabbath but the list is too long and some disagree with my definition of compelling. Anyway............ there is this priest that has become renowned of late. Many believe he saw a vision while practicing rituals within the Holy Place of the Temple. When he emerged after a prolonged time, he was unable to pronounce the customary blessing to the people for he was struck dumb – unable to speak! 8. (Luke 1:18-22)

He seemed likeable enough and I seriously doubt his priesthood is anything but devout. I have my reservations endorsing some others I have noticed taking liberties with the precepts of the Torah. But this Zachariah had defied the odds of chance and been selected to burn incense this particular morning. Lots are drawn to select this holy duty from among the twenty thousand priests vying for the opportunity. 7. (Luke 1:8-10) Some might contend that his fate, to be rendered speechless after receiving a vision, was conspicuously lacking admiration among those awaiting his blessing. His inability to communicate orally made his teaching 'utterly' impossible.

I subsequently heard that this elder priest returned home to his heretofore barren wife and conceived a child. And that instead of identifying him Zachariah II or some other elaborate family name, John was the carefully chosen given name. Apparently after this thunderstruck man of God conferred this name John to his son, he exploded in praise to God and prophesied the coming of a Savior who would redeem His people. His son John would prepare the way. 9 (Luke 1: 62-79)

My head is swimming with events of this year. Now a Messiah?

I must confess that the prospect of having our Davidic Kingdom restored, which by extension implies that the yoke of Roman oppression, mainly ridiculously high taxation, would be eliminated and is therefore very appealing. Wasn't it the prophet Nathan that delivered a message to David from the Lord that He "will raise up your offspring after you, who shall come from your body, and [the Lord] will establish his kingdom?

I guess it's kind of ironic that soon sons of David will be pouring into Bethlehem to be counted. I kind of doubt this baby John will be announcing anything momentarily. The kid should probably cut his teeth before any proclamation of here is the King of the Jews is expected. And these anticipated descendants of David have no army here in Israel. Of that I am quite certain.

Still...... I can revel in the prophecy and pray for this divination to transpire hurriedly. God's people have been subjected to many harsh and cruel foreign sovereigns for many years. Our faith could use a usurper. Some strong, formidable Jew to rally our kinsmen and drive the heathens from our lands.

My thoughts suddenly are redirected to the heathen Samaritan. His uncharacteristic display of compassion does not fit my metric for assigning contempt to this sect. But my pious nurture does not allow me the luxury of disregarding the multitude of sins I'm certain must be attributed to this ruffian, and I must condemn him.

And don't get me started on that doppelganger Herod the Great. King of the Jews? He's only half Jewish. He managed to rule with one foot in the Roman camp and the other within the Jewish holy city of Jerusalem that he restored to magnificence.

Hard to hate the guy though. Our economy is flourishing and prosperity is trickling down to all levels.

The Innkeeper's Story

Craftsmen have been busily constructing his palace, the Herodion. We have watched in amazement as a mountain top was removed and transported atop another higher peak to create an even more defensible position. And there's talk of a private villa, the Masada, being on the drawing boards. No one that wants to work is without an opportunity.

Herod's vision for Israel appears to incorporate the precepts of Judaism into the protection of the Roman Empire. This precarious balancing act is rife with Jewish criticism and yet Herod's iron grip on the Jewish guard is indisputable. He has already had three of his sons murdered, one of his wives, his mother-in-law and countless others he deemed conspirators against his regime. Either real or imagined.

Herod is the exact opposite of the Good Samaritan. Cruel. I, for one, will withdraw from any conversation belittling the king. His spy network is extensive and his mercy is nonexistent. Besides, I can attribute a steady flow of customers due to his industrial growth design for the city.

CHAPTER FIVE
No Room at the Inn

Young shepherd boy, Seth, has proven to be an excellent source of knowledge for selecting and procuring the animals needed for my inn. I continue to marvel at his animal acumen and lean on his advice. My thistle covered acreage is suitable for the sheep and goats and an insignificant pasture with a small brook is conveniently located on the property also.

I am hurriedly moving to finish the construction of the three new 'rooms' for the inn prior to the highly anticipated rush of occupants expected for the census registration. Some might interpret my kvetching as criticism. I prefer the disturbance to be considered naches, that sense of pride I feel when I add my kibitz. And by rooms, I mean those ten-by-ten-foot sections of limestone that I imagine to house six patrons each. A thin, straw mat will adequately define each person's expanse. And by expanse I really mean cramped quarters.

Bethlehem is bustling with immigrants here for the census. Every day pilgrims are making their trek, first here,

The Innkeeper's Story

and then on into Jerusalem. Lodging is so much more affordable here at my holiday inn than within the city walls. Six miles from Bethlehem can be traveled in two hours tops. A couple of hours for business and two more for temple. By the time you return to my inn, it's time to break bread. You save ten shekels.

My wife Bina is a huge support in my business endeavors. She has a shrewd sense of commerce and adjusts daily rates to reflect the supply and demand calculus. We are making a good living and concur that this was an astute move. Surprisingly we attribute the timing of the Samaritan's visit as the impetus for the decision to relocate.

The Samaritan and his compassionate anecdote are often a discussion between Bina and I. We cannot rationalize his actions. He obviously has been a target of ridicule and discrimination. Perhaps by the very Jew he has seemingly saved from a brutal death. Who's to say!

There is an unusual chill in the air nowadays. The winter solstice is making my daily routine somewhat chaotic. Shorter days and extended darkness tend to affect the mindset of my patrons and their hubris attitudes toward the inn management–namely me. They spend more time inside, and their incessant requests for my attention is annoying.

I have been enlightened to learn that the Romans have a coinciding solstice holiday, Saturnalia, the most popular holiday on the ancient Roman calendar. It is abounding with gifts and sacrifices for the winter harvest. I stand at

The Innkeeper's Story

the ready to eagerly partake of any Roman gift giving. It should be noted that I do not personally embrace their ritual but merely wish not to offend anyone that wishes to make me the benefactor of their benevolence.

Why should I stand in the way of their happiness?

Many of my guests are the tradesmen working on the upgrade of the Holy City. Masons, carpenters, polishers, weavers and other highly skilled craftsmen have found work there. Some of these laborers come from Roman communities.

We are at capacity tonight. If anything, I have overbooked. I have miscalculated the occupancy strategy providing for the current number of clients. People must literally step over or typically on other sojourners just to stretch or attend to personal business outside. It is not an optimum condition of hospitality, but the cha-ching of my coin purse assuages my guilt. And the service I render is not inconsequential. They are kept fed and warm. I have standards. It is just that my quality control matrix is a moving target.

Bina and I have completed our due diligence tonight. I have supplied our guests with the amenities we offer. Not so old wine and not so new blankets were distributed. I checked the stable area and conceded that Seth had been there previously and done an outstanding job of cleaning and mucking. He is more than likely huddled among his father's sheep on the nearby hillside.

Although sheep herding is not a vocation, I would never assume a synagogue teacher would ever suggest to a young aspiring student, it clearly was good enough for King David. 10.(1Samuel 16: 11-12) It is hard to dispute his lowly, smelly and dangerous upbringing and the dramatic impact this training had on defeating the Philistine giant Goliath. Hopefully God will bless Seth in a similar fashion one day. Perhaps Seth will bear witness to another miracle.

CHAPTER SIX
A BABE IS BORN

There is uneasiness tonight among the animals. The way a horse snorts and bucks when it senses a slithering. Or a hen nervously clucks and squawks if a fox nears. But my quick surveillance notices nothing out of place or obvious threat and I retreat back to the inn located a hundred cubits away.

It's not so much the distance I dread back to the inn as it is the expected rocky path that will ultimately result in bruised ankles or stubbed toes. Note to self: I really need to place oil lamps along the way to enhance the discernable formations of these obstacles. I am pleased to note though the unusually bright skyline and grin inwardly at my fortune tonight. Perhaps my trek will be less precarious. My gaze scans the path only, and I do not notice the images awaiting me at the inn.

I am suddenly alarmed by a panicky voice. His robe tacitly identifies this man as a Judean, and my immediate apprehension from his exclamations only intensifies as my gaze is drawn to his very pregnant wife sitting atop a mule.

The Innkeeper's Story

She is softly moaning. It's an understatement to suggest she is with child as she is obviously and immediately ready to deliver that child.

His insistence that they secure a room for the birth is more than problematic. There IS no room. Even Bina and I have conceded some of our privacy to share our quarters with three youngsters of registered guests.

I would confess that I am not as devout a Jew as I should be. I would even concede I have forgotten many precepts and principles supposedly 'learned' as a youngster in the synagogue. So, I was shocked and amazed that I suddenly recalled a passage from the Pentateuch, the book of Deuteronomy, that compelled us Jews to provide for our brothers in our land which the Lord your God has given you. And to freely and generously lend them sufficient for his need in whatever they lack.

That's not a section of the Torah that innkeepers try to memorize. Somewhat bad for business.

However, here I stand with a stark reality. My brother needs immediate privacy and I would argue more importantly a midwife. More accurately his wife needs one.

My mind is whirling with possibilities and then those are summarily discounted. My establishment is teeming with guests and even a few that require assistance to walk.

From the intensity of the audible discomfort our as yet unannounced visitor is producing, I'm guessing further accommodation considerations will become unnecessary in a matter of moments. I motion to follow me and incredibly he complies. The sure-footed animal obediently arrives with his human cargo without any unfortunate event and dutifully kneels to expedite her removal from his back.

The fresh straw seems to attract both the donkey and the pair of sojourners as they all gingerly make their way to the fragrant, soft bales in the corner by the manger. I nervously yell to them that I am going to get the swaddling and enlist the services of my wife. Even as I make my hasty exit, I conclude that I have made the best decision.

Bina is not without experience in birthing and has lent her talent in this capacity culminating in at least a dozen successful deliveries. Not surprisingly Bina has a clean supply of swaddling material at the ready and hastily retrieves it along with a cord and blade. My apprehension is only heightened by the prospect of being present for the pending procedure. I lead the way hoisting the oversized, lighted candle and become perplexed at the obvious illumination emitting from the stable. The aura is lustrous. And as we enter the stable the sensation of purity permeates to our core. There is no further need for the insignificant candle I possess. It's as though a focused beam of virtue has encapsulated the scene of mother and father.

Bina, too, is focused on what needs to transpire to protect mother and imminent child. She swiftly positions Mary. I can now refer to her by name as I have overheard the father discuss how he might comfort her.... this mother Mary. My furtive glance at Bina and subsequent waving of her hand assuages my angst as she silently dismissed me from the occasion. I am all too content to retreat outside.

I begin to ponder the future of this child being born in a stable. What will life be like? Perceptibly poor parents I concluded. Not an auspicious beginning. My thoughts are dramatically interrupted as the imperative shrieks of the newborn bore witness to his first breaths.

The obligatory need to congratulate the new parents leads me back inside the stable and finds everyone in good rapport. The exuberant father comforting and caressing the mother Mary and the swaddled baby resting comfortably in the manger. Bina is dutifully gathering up the vestiges of another natal success. The curiously well-behaved animals lingering nearby were also compliant.

Then curiously an entourage of shepherds appear at the cave. Seth is among them. And for the first time I am aware of the source of the fixated light. It's a star! Shining a light that is directed at the genesis of tonight. How can this be? What can it signify?

This motley crew of shepherds has been directed, they say, by an angelic visage to this place. They have been told that a Savior is born. Christ the Lord. The long-awaited Messiah.

This is incomprehensible! THE Messiah! The Promised Deliverer of the Jewish nation?

The One given authority, glory and sovereign power; all nations and peoples of every language will worship Him.

His dominion is an everlasting dominion that will not pass away and His kingdom is one that will never be destroyed!

A soft steady drumming is integrated into this extraordinary scene. Seth is effortlessly creating music on his daraba and the melodic rhythm is providing a cadence for rest. The baby is responding by wriggling deeper into the swaddling. The faintest smile appears on his mouth.

Many of this entourage have stayed the night watching the divine child asleep in a manager. Others have hastened to spread the story of this miraculous birth to anyone they encounter. Our very souls are filled with a heretofore unfelt tranquility. We seem incapable of separating ourselves from the baby.

CHAPTER SEVEN
THE IMMEDIATE FUTURE

The first rays of daylight seem to signal that even a miracle child must be fed as the baby releases significantly loud screams that it is also our cue to leave. I motion Joseph to accompany me outside the cave serving as the stable refuge. He acknowledges my request and offers a small purse with coins. Ostensibly for using the stable. My mouth becomes parched as my eyes widen and my head shakes back and forth in an effort to rebuke his effort to pay me.

I am suddenly wracked with guilt having to admit that I was unprepared to provide a more suitable accommodation for this nativity. They say Jewish guilt comes from ancestry. Tonight, was the total manifestation of that ism. I failed miserably in every conceivable hospitality.

I find myself imploring his family to stay with us. I promise to find a much more suitable living quarters for his wife and child and insist I won't take no for an answer. I can even offer him work. His carpentry skills are coveted, and I certainly have a need as we survey the half-finished rooms nearby.

I stopped short of bribing him to remain but I confess that was my next strategy. I do not want to bid farewell to this newfound joy and excitement his child has brought into our lives. Joseph surprisingly concurs that staying a short time is in the best interests of his newborn and young wife. They will remain and he will provide the carpentry.

It is impossible to convey how the next months of our existence were blessed by being in the presence of purity. It's as if any decision one makes is first run through a filter of love. Am I my brother's keeper? Will this bring happiness to those impacted by my action? Am I being fair and promoting this sense of phileo, this deep level of human connection. Instantly I am reminded of my encounter years ago with a man who also showed goodwill toward his fellowman. That Good Samaritan. He made the unpopular decision to follow a moral precept of philanthropy instead of a cultural bias. I can now imagine the bliss he received from such an action.

We are all God's creation. That Truth is heavy, so few men carry it.

It is a three-hour trek to Jerusalem from our inn. It is incumbent for every male child to participate in the circumcision ceremony eight days after their birth. This rite symbolized the special Jewish relationship with God.

Bina, Seth and I accompanied them to this ceremony as worship has now become a more conspicuous

The Innkeeper's Story

component of our lives. Our mules are surefooted and up for the burden of carrying the women and baby.

We celebrated as the rabbi officially named him Jesus, meaning 'to deliver', and praised God for his life. The trip back to Bethlehem was a joyous journey.

All these months later have also been marked by that abnormal, translucent star. Its light is no longer isolated on the nativity site but rather diffused over the town. The widened illumination apparently is highlighting our small population. Both Bina and I grudgingly conclude the explicit reason for the lingering radiance is attributable to the exalted child and not the worldly inhabitants of Bethlehem.

Joseph and Mary have settled into the mundane of raising a family. I am very pleased with the craftsmanship that Joseph provides as he labors tirelessly transforming wood into fine pieces of furniture. His carpentry skills are precise and proper. Mary is the ever-dutiful mother of a precocious child. Her own young years belie the maturity she exhibits when teaching the formative infant Jesus.

To state the obvious, Bina and I have witnessed amazing occurrences associated with the unique baby Jesus. It then perhaps should not have astonished us when a caravan of sage wise men knocked on the inn door. That translucent light was now once again beaming--highlighting the very space occupied by Mary and Joseph and Jesus. That pure emanation of enlightenment was focused on this young lad.

The Innkeeper's Story

These sagacious men of the east have been led to this child following this star for months and have come to honor and worship him. To bestow gifts worthy of a king producing gold, incense and myrrh. They fell prostrate at his feet and sang praises to Jesus in their own languages. It was glorious to watch the procession. 11.(Matthew 2:9-12)

This nobility was humbled in the presence of this child. Truly a king was born in my stable a few months ago. Who could refute the miraculous birth, the angelic light, the prophetic acclamation of Simeon in the Temple and now this explicit demonstration of homage from earthly royalty of distant lands?

This infant Jesus is the manifestation of the Messianic promise. As incredulous as it may be....He is standing in front of me.

The once barren hillside adjacent to the stable cave has now been transformed into a veritable fairground. Streaming silk canopies flap in the dusty breezes. Camels and peacocks attest to a faraway menagerie while servants attend to the luxurious trappings of monarchs.

Such a paradox! Earthly sovereigns paying homage to a mere child of humble means and as yet an unknown pedigree.

They are reluctant to leave his presence and are content to just bear witness to the fulfillment of the prophecy that the King of the Jews has arrived. Their arduous journey culminating in a most esteemed reverence and veneration.

CHAPTER EIGHT
The Flight

This morning has been a bit chaotic. Really? Can my life become more confused? What has transpired over these past months will never be consigned to any sense of normalcy! And yet, I observe a sudden hectic pace in dismantling the spectacle that served as the provisional quarters for the Magi. I suppose I always considered their stay as temporary, but such an abrupt departure surprises me.

Our hospitality was never predicated on an exaggerated bottom line of business but to be honest these extravagant visitors from afar have provided a generous addition to our coffers. And Seth has been busy providing lambs for meal preparation and hay and seed for their animals.

While lamenting their exodus from my property, I am suddenly aware that Joseph is beckoning me. He is standing among the Magi and talking in hushed tones as I approach.

The Magi quickly bow and hasten to the caravan that appears ready for departure. Joseph and I watch as this majesty disappear over the horizon and into the heat of another day. It dawns on me that their path is ill advised as the shortest route to the east, but who am I to offer unsolicited advice to such learned men?

Joseph slowly turns to me and his face is evidence of pending bad news. We have grown close. It has evolved into a friendship born of necessity but cultivated by trust and respect.

I am quickly told that it is incumbent for his family to relocate. That the child is now in danger of harm from among the ruling family. Ruthless men of power are certain to jeopardize his very life as they fully intend to disregard God's plan for mankind and to further their own ambitions. A prophetic child is still just a child and incapable of mustering an army. Until it isn't just a child. Eliminate the threat early and the uninterrupted order is maintained.

Therefore, Jesus and Mary will necessarily be relocated to Egypt. They now have the means. The Magi were generous. Joseph inquires if he may purchase suitable livestock for the trek as Cairo is over three hundred miles completed via many perilous roads.

I am on an emotional roller coaster. Stunned, saddened and supportive all at once. Who would dare to harm an innocent? Has humanity sunk so low that a child's life is deemed inconsequential to the sustaining of a puppet king?

Sickened! I am also sickened by his revelation.

I am curiously strengthened in my resolve to never let that happen. I will defend my new friend's family and as yet the uncrowned king of my people with everything at my disposal. My very life if required.

The Innkeeper's Story

And of course, Joseph may select the finest from among the livestock. I'll get Seth to assist.

In all my thirty-five years I have never been more compelled to provide for the well-being of my guests. My career is based on delivering the necessities necessary for a pleasant stay and now, by extension, in departing.

Joseph is hastily preparing the family's possessions for travel as Seth and I select the beasts most capable of completing the many weeks' excursion as the immediacy of departure is apparent. Tomorrow at dawn is deemed as the flight into Egypt exit.

Bina is heartsick too. She has prepared a final meal for our friends and has included Seth as he has not played an insignificant role in this miraculous adventure. Young Jesus sits and intently listens as once again Seth entertains us with his drumming. Prayers and Psalms are spoken for a safe journey and the anticipated someday reunion.

Daylight hastens! Goodbyes are abbreviated. A foreboding of lurking danger permeates. Another quick embrace of the King as tears well up and then trickle down my cheek. Seth will guide them to a shortcut used by shepherds that avoids all pedestrian traffic and more importantly the guards of the seated counterfeit ruler, King Herod.

The Joy that has been in Bethlehem is ebbing into the distance. So too is the holy light that has surrounded our little town. Extinguished by the departure of this sacred family.

The melancholy of the moment is rendered insignificant in only two short days with the appearance of palace soldiers. They enter homes without justification and seize infant male children to murder. 12.(Matthew 2:16-17) Mothers are inconsolable and screams of horror are echoed throughout the township as child after child is murdered.

It is a disastrous attempt to annihilate the Messiah, the infant Jesus. This must have been the vision of the Magi and Joseph and thus was the nexus for their spontaneous departure.

The depression that has enshrouded Bethlehem is palpable. Our inn was searched and rudely trashed looking for their intention. The guards press us for information as they hurl accusations regarding rumors that a family has been staying here matching the description of the pursued child. And while I have no intention of betraying them, I can honestly say, please look for yourself.

Seth arrives shortly after the soldiers withdraw from our establishment. He communicates that the family is enroute to Egypt via a route seldom used by anyone other than the Bedouins. Seth is confident that his friends will safely escort the family from tribe to tribe and conclude at the destination without peril. Sighs of relief are heard. Bina and I retreat within our inn to offer a thanksgiving prayer for them and a prayer of solace for the grieving mothers.

CHAPTER NINE
MY FATHER'S BUSINESS

A decade has elapsed since we have seen the sacred family but they are never far from our thoughts. Much has occurred in this interim. Perhaps most importantly our former despotic, maniacal pseudo-King Herod has perished.

Ravaged by his own lunacy and paranoia hopefully. While his replacements, his sons, weren't as meshuggener (crazy), they demonstrate psychotic symptoms and continue to defile God's laws and priests.

Imagine our delight when we are summoned to the cave that once served as the stable for our Messiah's birth and find the holy family awaiting us. Mary and Joseph and now this handsome lad of twelve, Jesus. All are smiling at Bina and me. They are traveling to Jerusalem for Jesus' confirmation.

Young Jewish men of this age should fulfill the requirement of the law. Their spiritual nature and understanding and knowledge of the Jewish law will be tested by the priests during a ceremony. This rite was intended to respectfully remove the responsibility of religious training from the parents to the young man himself. The Temple at Jerusalem must have been the most consecrated ground he has ever traveled to.

And while they cannot stay tonight perhaps, they could share a meal with us during their return to Nazareth in a few days. This gives us ample time to ensure a delightful banquet and more time to catch up on the past years in Egypt and Nazareth. I will make certain that Seth receives an invitation too. Seth has become quite the entrepreneur since he last saw the holy family. He will rejoice remembering that angelic encounter and subsequent welcoming of the child King Jesus.

The entourage that included the sacred family proceeded to Jerusalem a mere half day travel, but the massive crowds heading for the celebration Feast of the Passover restricted the speed of movement along the road. Doubling the intended time, it took to reach the city.

The Passover undoubtedly is the most important required jubilee which celebrated the exodus of Jews from Egypt. Throngs of travelers made this the busiest period for an innkeeper too as there was additionally the immediate Feast of Unleavened Bread. Wayfarers were desperate for accommodations. I was in the business of providing for this necessity.

Bina has prepared a delicious Seder dinner. There is a salty gefilte fish, a simmering matzo ball soup, a casserole stew of carrots and prunes and the symbolic charoset.

The Innkeeper's Story

Technically this meal proceeds the celebration of Passover but there was no time to extend this hospitality, and now we want to honor the blessed family of Jesus with this courtesy. Our imminent King of the Jews.

Visualize the ensuing chaos when the blessed Jesus is nowhere to be found among his family or extended company. A discernable panic results as questions regarding his last known location are answered with shrugs of disbelief and lament. Think, think! Who saw Jesus last? Was he ever amongst us when we left our camp in Jerusalem?

It is determined that Mary and Joseph will return to the city to expand the search. Seth will secure the assistance of his shepherd community to hunt along the outskirts between Bethlehem and Jerusalem in case Jesus has wandered away carelessly. Bina and I will focus our attention on the multitude passing by in case there is a chance he has been purposefully abducted and is among the conspirators. We are made anxious by our reflection on the massacre of the innocents associated with the brutal effort to kill Jesus all those years ago. Could another assassination attempt explain his disappearance?

Days hence we learn the reality. Our frenetic fear was misplaced and replaced with enlightened awe. This most important festival of Passover would have assembled the most learned rabbis from around Israel who unquestionably would have been discussing the coming Messiah as a popular topic. The young, precocious Jesus was discovered intently listening and asking probing questions of these scholars in the temple court. His confirmation transition from parental instruction to personal responsibility for religious training was apparent.

Mary was frantically looking for a boy. She found a bahur (young man). She was admonished by Jesus to relinquish her maternal instincts and let him exercise a more compliant path of wisdom and understanding of God's will for his life. 13. (Luke 2: 41-50) I never saw the holy family again throughout my midlife.

CHAPTER TEN
JORDAN JOURNEY

Decade's pass. Work at our inn prospers as pilgrims to Jerusalem stop for the night to avoid the higher lodging fees escalated by the proximity to the city proper. Bina and I are ever pressing our guests for news of a prophet in Israel. Most queries are met with looks of skepticism and cynicism. After all, there hasn't been a legitimate prophet of God for over four hundred years. Why on earth expect one now? But we are convinced that the Messiah Jesus is biding His time and will ascend to the throne shortly and remove the yoke of Roman oppression and deliver us from the shackles of bondage.

My family is content in the knowledge that Jesus is walking among us on earth. And that He will manifest himself as God's intended king of Israel soon. Moses and Elijah and father Abraham surely became God's future revelation to men but for some divine reason only poor shepherds and foreigners realize that the King of the Jews has already been born. I desire to witness the coronation of Jesus before I pass. I want to die a free man of Israel.

The Innkeeper's Story

I recently heard a teaching by our priest from the Pentateuch book of Numbers. This Torah passage implied that our Lord God engaged Moses to direct men of thirty years of age among the Kohathite tribe to work in the Tent of Meeting. This tabernacle or miskan (dwelling place) was the temporary accommodation place for the Ark of the Covenant and the other holy items.

Curiously I also recall within the book of Genesis that Jacob's son Joseph was thirty years old when he began serving the patriarch of Egypt. And that King David began his reign of Judah at thirty. Okay, okay maybe I'm connecting dots that don't exist. But I did do the calculus and concluded that Jesus' age is within this time frame.

There is an old Jewish quote from Proverbs: "Gray hair is a crown of glory; It is attained by the way of righteousness." I have thus been crowned. My time grows closer.

Our country is oppressed. The Romans have taxed us beyond reason and the heir of Herod the Great aka Herod Antipas, his son, is just as corrupt as was his father. He panders to the Romans and has little concern for governing fairly and only for lining his own pockets with graft and immoral living. It is an unspoken truth that he has married his half-brother's wife. A violation of the Mosaic law.

And don't get me started on the Sanhedrin. This assemblage of imaginary piety is also vain and suspiciously wealthy. How can priests charged with serving the temple become independently affluent? They appear way too cozy with the political authority vested by Rome in Judaea.

The Innkeeper's Story

This trickle-down economics they practice apparently has become but a mere mist by the time it reaches the working poor. They pray for the promised Messiah, and yet I sense their rationale is so they can become even more authoritative as His favored priests during his reign.

Bina has cautioned me to withhold my personal biases for fear of reprisal. She opines that my unsubstantiated assertions will travel along the network of local priestly Sanhedrin doppelgangers and ultimately gain the attention of those willing to protect this organization by any methods at their disposal. You tend to lose inhibitions at my age. Also, good sense it seems to Bina.

A recent visitor to our inn regaled us with an interesting and thought-provoking story. It seems during his travel he encountered a baptizer along the Jordan River. This man's preaching was totally controversial and demanded repentance for sins even from the king himself. He was teaching that judgement was at hand and no one would escape God's verdict. His blistering sermons called out graft, blackmail and hypocrisy and expected those listening to him to admit and renounce their guilt and to be reborn anew via baptism into a new loving ideology.

He was pronounced a prophet by the crowds who eagerly entered into a wilderness to seek his words and be baptized by him. His antiestablishment rhetoric and his obvious convictions of necessary repentance were keys to every sermon. This man of meager means was soon deemed to have come in the spirit and power of Elijah.

The Innkeeper's Story

A noteworthy characteristic since Malachi asserted that Elijah will return "before that great and dreadful day of the Lord."

No wonder throngs of people were listening to this voice of one calling: "In the desert prepare the way for the Lord, make straight in the wilderness for our God." I must make this journey too.

The clamor that a prophet is preaching in the wilderness has reached our town. This must be Jesus! He is beseeching men and women to renounce their sins and repent. His attire belies the accessories of a king though. Seems people are reporting this prophet is dressed in a tunic of camel hair. 14. (Matthew 3:4-7) And while this is a valued, simple garment that protects from blazing desert sun and offers warmth in the cold nights, one associates the purple cloths with the station of a king. Surely the Messiah of the Jews, their king, is so worthy.

I must venture into the desert to see my king once more before I pass. I am giddy with excitement to reunite with him and often contemplate as to whether Jesus will recall our brief but miraculous visits. Bina and I will recruit Seth to manage the inn while we sojourn to a questionable area around the Jordan River where apparently he preaches most often.

Seth has been a son to us. Not unlike us, his life was transformed after the visitation of the angels at Jesus' birth. He has grown in the realization that he was blessed beyond measure to witness that miracle so many years ago. His life became one of kindness and mercy and worship. He continues to compose songs of praise to Yahweh that he shares with our village. This dear man has been a blessing to Bina and me especially as our diminishing stamina takes a toll.

The prophet was purported to be located south of Jerusalem along the Jordan. Ergo we set off along the rocky roads toward that portion of the river merging frequently with other wayfarers compelled to hear this man "crying in the wilderness" too.

Around the campfires at night, we are intrigued by the conversations regarding the similarities in description between the prophet Elijah and the baptizer we are headed to see. It was particularly interesting to note that Elijah too wore a garment of hair and a leather belt around his waist.

The actual distance to the Jordan belies the time it takes for Bina and I to travel there. Our deliberate pace does not exact too much exertion upon our frail bodies and permits us to thoroughly enjoy the vista that God has bestowed in this the Promised Land of the Jewish nation. Perhaps our King Jesus will restore our legacy before I pass.

Jesus, our long-awaited Messiah, is here on earth. Perhaps just over the next ridge! The throngs of people anxious to hear and see him are jockeying for the best vantage points from atop this bluff. Many fellow Jews are asking us if they can assist in our quest to negotiate the incline and gently guide us to the superior ground. Our gratitude is expressed in our smiles as our heavy breathing conflicts with speaking actual words of thanks.

The Innkeeper's Story

When our eyes have adjusted to the glare associated with the desert sand and the noonday reflection from the river, we notice a disheveled man standing hip deep in the river. This man is not my Jesus.

He looks more like someone possessed and sounds like someone with a death wish since his impetuous message shouted for all to overhear is denouncing the current Jewish ruler, Herod Antipas, rebuking him for divorcing his wife and unlawfully wedding Herodias, his sister-in-law.

His message seemed to segue from the immorality of Herod to the need of repentance for all men. He demanded regret for sinning against God and asserted that judgement was at hand and the kingdom of heaven nearby. He proceeded to baptize all whom heard and then expressed a desire to be born again symbolized by the heartfelt act of immersion beneath the muddy Jordan reemerging to a new life devoted to serving God and their fellow mankind.

John's message of 'do penance: for the kingdom of heaven is at hand' resonated within the residents of Jerusalem and Judea. His mandate for generosity 'giving coats and meat' to those not having either, denounced anyone who was selfish and dishonest to this proposition.

Hundreds among the crowd felt compelled to renounce their sinful ways and dutifully entered into the Jordan to be immersed by this John the Baptizer. Their fervor to join other kindred minds in John's spiritual movement was manifest by a rejoicing echoed by all devotees of John.

Prophet John was also extoling another. One who he claimed was the Lamb of God, the Son of God–the long-awaited Messiah.

This man was truly a prophet from God, but he was not my Jesus, the Messiah.

From our lofty vantage point Bina and I could clearly hear and witness John preaching and baptizing. Suddenly our eyes locked on a most handsome, self-confident man wading into the shallows of the Jordan to approach the prophet. A visceral gasp escaped from our mouths. A quick, furtive glance was exchanged between us that somehow confirmed our mutual belief that this commanding figure was indeed our Jesus. Our basis for identification was not necessarily a recognition of physical features, for it had been two decades since we last beheld his youthful face, but rather an immediate instinctual connection with one so endowed with an undeniable purity and demonstrable attitude of majesty.

This man WAS my Jesus!

Why was he then entering into this ceremony, and by ceremony, I mean into the filthy Jordan, that ostensibly was symbolically intended to denounce a sinful life?

An apparent kerfuffle ensued as Jesus approached the baptizer but then Jesus disappeared and shortly emerged from the water. In the next moment our senses were confounded. The very sky appeared to open as clouds were separated and a drenched Jesus stood with hands clasped looking up and praying. A blast of sheer energy appeared

The Innkeeper's Story

to encompass Jesus and a glorious aura superseded the light of a noonday sun. This glory light must have been similar to the event that our friend Seth witnessed at the birth of Jesus.

Seth used to enthrall us with his account of angels announcing the location of Jesus' birthplace and entreating the shepherds to pay homage even as the shepherds trembled in abject fear. I was beginning to commiserate with that anxiety.

And now as if by some divine intervention a dove gently settles upon Jesus 15. (Matthew 3:16) and a din that defied any explanation that I might offer was heard by those in attendance but without interpretation. These perplexing moments were inadequately described by me even days later.

Suffice it to say that Bina and I only marginally resisted the temptation to race down the slope to be likewise joined in the association of baptism. The racing descriptor was a matter of perspective but not the public declaration of repentance we both now desired. We wanted to be more like Jesus!

Our quest to see Jesus culminated with our spiritual healing. In our unqualified failed attempt, to somehow entertain Jesus with our conceited admiration and leverage our own puny passing acquaintance, we were instead to become true disciples of his good news. John's message urged us to deny our selfish desires and to practice mercy

The Innkeeper's Story

and love instead. Every so often I have a recurrence of how that good Samaritan so long ago demonstrated such virtue.

We returned to our inn rejoicing in our decision to believe in the Lamb of God and to strive to abandon our self-centeredness.

CHAPTER ELEVEN
Teachings from Jesus

The inn was always a convergence of ethnicities, of differing religious philosophies and a bounty of newsflashes as visitors to Jerusalem chatted at the dinner buffet Bina provided nighty. The rule of Roma was a conspicuous topic as their empire expanded eastward from Italia and now included the occupation of Israel. From Egypt to Syria people were oppressed and heavily taxed to support the military expansion. Very few of our boarders were sympathetic to the animus exhibited by these occupiers. Rumors of outright rebellion were made public quickly followed by cautionary tales of implementation. Crucifixion was the Roman preferred method of punishing slaves and those guilty of sedition. The pain would have been excruciating with the added insult of humiliation. It would serve as a massive deterrent to anyone with the common sense to see past any illegality in the contradiction of Roman sovereignty.

Mixed in among the régime gossip were stories of Jesus. He was purported to have enlisted common men into his

The Innkeeper's Story

tribe of disciples, and they were touring the countryside healing and teaching tolerance among men and service to Yahweh. Jesus was astonishing the priests and rabbis with his knowledge and interpretation of the Torah wherever he worshiped.

He pointed out hypocrisy and ignorance of the law to these learned priests thereby eroding their influence and station among the people. The obvious consequence was disgust and distain for the carpenter from Nazareth. Yet they secretly marveled at his inexplicable ability to heal the sick. Rumors of their desire to discredit and denounce this prophet quickly surfaced while the cheers and the adoration of Jesus deafened their false accusations of heresy. 16. (Luke 4:18-20, 28)

Bina and I found ourselves beseeching new lodgers for any news of the exploits of our Jesus. His fame and formidable presence were usurping the office and rank of the religious elite. His messages of love were resonating with the community wherever he preached but served to aggravate the religiousness of the most pious who equated compassion with weakness.

One evening we were astounded by a narrated story shared by a guest. While not a member of the twelve-disciple assembly, he was an avid follower of Jesus and related having been instructed by Jesus to visit towns outside Capernaum and to prepare them for Jesus' later visit. What a blessing he claimed! Pairs of men had done miraculous things in the name of Jesus – healing and witnessing. The

The Innkeeper's Story

seventy-two reported back to Jesus and his disciples with joy and proclaimed their success, noting that even demons had submitted to His name. They then bore witness to a story of love shared by Jesus to the twelve and an interested lawyer.

The lawyer posited to Jesus the question: What must I do to inherit eternal life? Evidently it is true that lawyers never ask questions not already knowing the expected answer and responded to Jesus' query about what the Law says in the Torah correctly. You must love the Lord your God with all your soul and with all your strength and with all your mind, and Love your neighbor as yourself he replied.

Jesus concurred and admonished him to truly do this and he would live. Yet the lawyer was not convinced of the parameters of this definition of neighbor and further inquired as to just who was his neighbor.

Now it's the next part of our new friend and lodger's story that left both Bina and me wide-eyed, for then Jesus tells how a Samaritan man found this half dead Jew alongside the road and took mercy on him. Apparently, a priest and a Levite had noticed this wounded countryman, but instead of helping, quickly moved to the other side of the road in a failed attempt to assuage their guilt for refusing aid. However, this Samaritan, an anathema to sincere Jews, exhibited mercy and compassion and arranged to have this injured traveler cared for at an inn. He even advanced payment for necessary attention to this injured man. 17.(Luke 10:30-37)

What?! Bina and I stared at the disciple. We were incredulous. Jesus had all but identified us as characters in his analogy. It was our inn. We had dealt with the Samaritan and have marveled for years at that episode and now to hear that our Lord knows of that encounter and uses it to promote common mercy was astonishing. Praise be to God.

The next several months around our inn were filled with conversations relating the exploits of our Lord Jesus the Messiah witnessed or recanted by our guests at the inn. He was once preaching to multitudes along the Sea of Galilee and somehow feeds this massive crowd of over five thousand. He calms raging storms, cleanses a man of leprosy, heals the lame, restores sight to the blind, and even reportedly walked on water. How can anyone but God the Messiah do these miracles?

We are a changed family too. We know the mercy and love Jesus extended to us and have vowed via baptism and personal confession to be more like Jesus. Bina and I and even Seth have committed our lives to serving as disciples of Jesus. Our actions are driven by our desire to reflect his love to all, even our neighbors of Samaria, our long-held enemies of Israel. And although the Romans may control our government, they cannot control our hearts. We will pray for our adversaries. We will serve the King of the Jews.

The Innkeeper's Story

It is incredulous to us that our Sanhedrin Hebrew piety counsel has not conveyed upon Jesus the feature of King of the Jews too. Some even appear to possess an animosity toward Jesus and speak out in the temple against him mentioning some miracles as works of the devil. The denounce Jesus for healing on the Sabbath. For healing a fellow Jew they became upset?

Why won't they acknowledge his divinity? Jealousy perhaps?

CHAPTER TWELVE
THE KINGLY COLT

Our Inn is prospering. Rooms have been added. Livestock continues to multiply. My age and associated maladies handicap my ability to keep up with all the demands and rigors of the ensuing maintenance. The door to success is marked "push" and "pull" according to a Jewish proverb. I have necessarily enlisted the services of Seth more and more. He is surely the son Bina and I have shrewdly assumed.

Seth has a gift with animals that was probably made superior mostly due to his heritage among the shepherds. This innate aptitude extends to all our animal assemblage. Seth's reputation in husbandry has made him somewhat of an expert among his fellow nomads of the desert too. His acumen translating into hardier and more beautiful varieties of creatures. His breeding techniques are fascinating science.

Only today has he acknowledged the birth of a new breed of donkey or colt. A colt is a young male donkey which is less than four years of age. The colt he divulges is

The Innkeeper's Story

pure white. The rarest color among the donkeys. Apparently, a sojourner from the Roman province of Gallia Aquitania was making a pilgrimage to Jerusalem and was hauling tradecraft via mules he had shipped to Joppa when he serendipitously ran into Seth in the market outside the gates of Jerusalem. Seth too was bartering his sought-after sheep as they struck a conversation regarding the complexities of creating superior strands of livestock both acknowledging the more enhanced versions each was currently displaying.

The tradesman presented a mutual contract. An esteemed donkey for four of Seth's prized sheep. A firm handshake had sealed the deal.

This new hybrid donkey colt was stunning. The stark coloration overwhelmed the logic of this anomaly and strained the veracity of the obvious. Instead of a typical grayish, hairy and of dubious personality donkey there was a beautiful, white and even regal worthy one. The incongruity between the two would have been as apparent as comparing a lump of gold found in the river and a rock from the same sandy bottom. One was far more appealing and precious.

Seth had managed to create a conundrum for himself though. Hiding a valuable assay of gold is somewhat doable. Concealing a moving beast that presumably will only grow and become more noticeable isn't practical. He adroitly realizes his prize will be confiscated and his anticipated treasure will be appropriated. I give it less than

The Innkeeper's Story

six months before news of this existence has unintended consequences.

Seth lives within a small nomadic village comprised mostly of shepherds just east of Bethpage closer to Jerusalem that Bethlehem. Over these many years Bina has prudently engaged Seth for all variety of tasks within our commerce. His judgment and shrewd choices have proven invaluable to us time and time again. Seth has been an integral part of our family ever since that first noel and has matured into the sensible man and devoted follower of Jesus not unlike my family. He does however maintain an allegiance to the shepherd community and chooses to make his home inside this tight knit assembly.

His prized colt and donkey are attracting attention among the public, and his efforts to breed a more desirable and sturdier beast of burden were receiving rave reviews. This colt had a beautiful white coloration except for the usual marking resembling two intersecting lines between the eyes of the animal. A feature that Seth believes is a flaw that can be eliminated with future offspring. I tell Seth it's just an amusing design, to spare his feelings, but it somewhat reflects the cruel cross structure used by Romans to crucify their detractors, traitors and anyone who dares to challenge the authority. Let's hope no one else lets their mind wander to that comparison. That might be bad for business.

CHAPTER THIRTEEN
POWER OVER DEATH

Meanwhile the scarcity of news regarding Jesus has been replaced by the constant regaling of his achievements. Thousands are seeking his presence. His esteem has grown even more quickly than anyone in the country and has placed him at odds with the priesthood who claim a bloodline to Aaron the brother of Moses. These Levites find their sphere of influence eroding among the worshipers and they are none too happy. These three years of teaching and healing in the name of God have made Jesus the ultimate Jewish authority within the Temple and among the people.

I must confess that I contemplate the timing associated with when Jesus will announce his kingdom to all Jews and Romans and assume the throne. His mighty prowess has been demonstrated over and again. We humbly praise his virtue and blissfully await his demonstration of military acumen necessary to overthrowing the shackles of slavery imposed upon us by the Romans. As God's chosen race, we temper the love Jesus has espoused with the destiny of

The Innkeeper's Story

armed aggression. How else will he be crowned the King of the Jews? Blood will be shed. I see no voluntary surrender as a viable option being considered by the haughty Romans.

Word has spread like a wildfire among the olive trees that Jesus has raised a man of Bethany from the dead. A man named Lazarus had become ill and died. He had been dead for four days before Jesus came at the request of Mary and Martha the sisters of this devoted follower of the Christ.

By all witness accounts Jesus looked unto heaven and thanked God for sending him to love and help his people and then shouted for this corpse to emerge from a cavern tomb. They marveled as he exited still bound in his grave clothes of linen. The many friends of the family that were there to comfort the sisters and who witnessed this miracle now put their faith in Jesus and became devoted followers. My Jesus has the power over life and death. 18.(John 11:43-45)

CHAPTER FOURTEEN
THE JERUSALEM INN HAS AN UPPER ROOM

My inn is continuously at capacity with guests seeking to see or hear Jesus. Sojourners throughout Judea are heading for Jerusalem. They know that the Passover is a festival Jesus will attend and are eager to even glimpse this man of God and they must have a place to sleep. My inn meets that need. The relentless kvetching among the overcrowded boarders is easily ignored by me.

My blessings are continual and my purse grows heavy. It's not as if my business acumen has increased. It's more like God is consecrating and directing my corporate decisions as my belief and faith in Jesus grows and produces undeniable devotion and commitment to do what God wants.

Case in point. An aristocratic landowner/innkeeper inside Jerusalem suddenly desired to visit his ailing relatives in Capernaum. He did not trust those working for him to be honest while he was away and implored Bina

The Innkeeper's Story

and I to manage his property in his absence. We negotiated a generous contract knowing the likelihood of providing available Passover holiday accommodations inside the city was a financial certainty. I will divide my time between Bethlehem and Jerusalem until my friend returns. I feel compelled to accept this offer as though being directed by a higher power.

While serving as the interim host concierge in Jerusalem, I have become acquainted with the tenants that maintain a presence here for an extended period of time. Many are high ranking priests or members of the Sanhedrin, a powerful religious and political body. They reside in Jerusalem while conducting business and then return home to manage their personal wealth.

I attempt to maintain a polite social separation and busy myself anticipating their next essential need, which is usually nothing more than self-indulgence. I must confess occasionally to eavesdropping on sensitive and controversial topics discussed among this elite at meal time. I have concluded the vast majority of this august body is more concerned with how Jesus' teachings of love and compassion are juxtaposed to theirs of political expediency and spiritual law. Only one man has endeavored to interpret Jesus promises and teachings as perhaps messianic prophecy. This man, Joseph of Arimathea, is also the inn's richest client and has reserved the entire upper room for the duration of his stay in Jerusalem. Perhaps that is why the other resident Pharisees become mute while he

The Innkeeper's Story

presents an alternative theory recommending Jesus as the promised Messiah.

Admittedly I cannot suppress my admiration for this fellow follower of Jesus and sometimes contribute an Amen at opportune moments of concurrence during his defense of my Jesus. It is met with looks of contempt from the majority gathered, and I dutifully withdraw my personal presence from the room ostensibly to attend to another menial task intended to make their lives better.

This Joseph of Arimathea has the pedigree and providence to command in any audience. His acute knowledge of prophecies and discernment are exactly the characteristics we laymen of Jesus disciples desire among our priests.

CHAPTER FIFTEEN
The Palms

Bina and I will be extremely busy this week. It is the Passover! Extra stores must be secured. An innkeeper must accommodate to provide for any circumstance that benefits the boarder. And now we are split in our support as Bina is solely responsible for the Bethlehem inn, and I now have been challenged to maintain the Jerusalem guesthouse per my agreement.

The Passover is quite a festive occasion that foreshadowed the exodus of Jewish captivity from Egyptian bondage. A Feast of Unleavened Bread is included within the week and our guests expect tender lamb, the finest wine they can afford and the freshest bread albeit without the yeast. Seth will provide us the lambs while wine merchants are easily found among the vendors. I will pay additional attention and detail to the rich, religious leader Joseph of Arimathea who will undoubtedly provide a generous gratuity for such a courtesy.

We have exhibited a tacit respect for one another having bonded by our relationship with Jesus.

The Innkeeper's Story

The commotion of excited Jews entering the city was expected. But the current cacophony suggested the arrival of royalty. Who commanded such a substantial welcome? My guests obviously were just as inquisitive and abandoned their meals, their serious conversations or restful tranquility to hurry toward the turbulent demonstration.

Hurry being the operative and subjective word was me being many paces behind the exiting clients and becoming a mere addition to the swelling throng of peoples. Yet I was present when the multitude began shouting: "Hosanna! Blessed is the king who comes in the name of the Lord! Peace in Heaven. Glory in the highest!" Words very similar echoed in my mind as I recalled the birth of Jesus years ago. The shepherds testified to angels appearing and praising God saying, "Glory to God in the highest, and on earth Peace to men.

Palm branches were now being waved back and forth and cloaks were being shed to throw in front of.........Seth's colt and donkey? On the back of his unmistakable white donkey 19.(Judges 5:10) was my Lord Jesus. The fervor of the crowd was palpable. Hysteria was the rule as Jesus' disciples joyfully praised God in delirious voices for all the miracles they had seen over the years. One could not escape the undeniable passion that captivated the crowd.

My heart swelled with joy as I watched Jesus enter into the Holy City of Jerusalem in fulfillment of yet another messianic prophecy promoted by Zechariah, "See, your king comes to you, righteous and having salvation, gentle

The Innkeeper's Story

and riding on a donkey." And I was beaming with pride as I saw a grinning Seth leading the foal.

I could hardly wait to hear how this regal procession had incorporated this poor shepherd. 20. (Mark 11: 1-6) My thoughts recollected how Seth played on his daraba (drum) that first noel to soothe the livestock and pacify the infant baby Jesus. Now a grown man and a follower of Jesus, he was once again able to honor his king with a gift of love.

But upon further notice of the burgeoning crowd, it became apparent that not everyone was joyously celebrating the triumphant entry of Israel's king into the city. Disgruntled, even disdainful, squints were obvious among the piety gathered along the road. It was hard for me to reconcile their reaction to such a marvelous occasion. Why weren't they leading this pageant? Surely, they knew of the prophecies and had witnessed Jesus' miracles! How could anyone doubt the authenticity of this man being the legitimate Messiah? A conundrum not shared by those cheering Jesus now as he passed into the Holy City.

CHAPTER SIXTEEN
Passover Preparation

The Feast of the Unleavened Bread was nigh. Preparations were completed and rendered acceptably suitable by the host, guest Joseph of the Jewish Council. The inn's upper room has been reserved for his convenience throughout this week and I strive mightily to insure his approval.

As time and schedule permit, we share stories we have either personally witnessed or collected from other believers involving the exploits of our king, Lord Jesus. He is mesmerized by my accounting of the fateful noel in my stable. He insists on my recollection of the details. How many animals, shepherds, angels? Alas I am testifying to only my perspective and woefully describe that miracle. He doesn't care and wants only to listen and smile.

He shares the many occasions he has listened to Jesus preach. Once he was instructed on a hillside with thousands of others as our Lord laid out how we were to treat our fellowman. And how his heart was bursting with happiness from hearing those words. He witnessed Jesus blessing a few loaves and fishes and giving them to the disciples to distribute to the masses. And how baskets were needed to collect the leftovers. He admitted to wanting to become a disciple too like Peter, James and John and follow Jesus everywhere. He confides that he will soon publicly pronounce Jesus as King of the Jews.

Now my attention must be redirected to the Feast. I cannot find the attendant and must grudgingly assume the menial and typically feminine chore of bringing fresh water to the inn from the nearby communal well. Giggles are overheard from among the female contingency as I hoist the jar onto my shoulder and slosh much of the water as I make my way. Perhaps the snickers could also be attributed to the fact this jar is half the size foisted by the women. My bruised ego will survive.

Quite unexpectedly I noticed two of Jesus disciples hurriedly approaching. I recognized the one with the unusually large hands and scruffy beard as the fisherman Peter. The other disciple was much less disheveled and was introduced as John. I was astounded to learn that they intended to follow me as they had noted I was the only man lugging water. 21(Luke 22:10)

So? I'm certain I wasn't the only gent that had had to succumb to this task today. Ummm if you are headed in my direction, perhaps a helping hand? Now who looks ridiculous!! We innkeepers are a creative community.

I lead this small entourage to the inn and am shocked that Joseph suddenly and unexpectedly appears in the

The Innkeeper's Story

doorway as though intended by providence. Peter unabashedly presents the request to Joseph: "The Teacher asks: Where is the guest room, where I may eat the Passover with my disciples?"22. (Luke 22: 11-12)

To my utter confoundment and without hesitation, Joseph leads the duet to the chamber I've been prepping for the pending seder. Peter and John are seemingly duly impressed with my groundwork and tacitly express approval with nods. A few additional pillows are requested along with the assurance that enough bread and wine will be provided. Joseph turns to me and raises his eyebrows to query my guarantee that this entreaty will indeed be assured. A humble bow is my response.

Will my Lord be celebrating here tonight? I wanted to interrogate these disciples. May I impose and join this momentous meal? Is Jesus' arrival in Jerusalem the signal for announcing his kingship? Will another star decree his Messianic reign? Angels glorify him as the Savior once more?

Maybe this pair didn't know that Jesus and I have a unique bond. It's my duty I think to educate them to this circumstance. And perhaps leverage this condition to gain access to the commemorative "order".

I inaudibly withdraw and hasten to assure that requested trappings are secured. Pillows are not going to be an issue but I'm now second guessing my choice of wine to serve to our Master. Plus, I must inform Bina of this glorious situation. Jesus will be here tonight and ostensibly proclaiming himself as the Son of God and assume the throne to lead his people from the oppressive servitude of Roman rule. God's people will again rejoice that the promise land given to father Abram will be unrestricted by foreign influence.

What better time for this holy declaration! I doubt tonight's ritual seder celebration of deposing Egyptian bondage is coincidental to Jesus assuming Jewish kingship to eliminate the current Roman captivity. The previous miracles performed by my lord Jesus attest to the brevity of the pending conflict with the Romans. Most certainly he will dispatch them with at least as much decisiveness as Moses did the Egyptians. Plagues, boils, hail, locusts or angels of death seem all too likely to resurface soon.

I am troubled that Seth has always insisted that the angelic proclamation of Jesus' birth included the phrase, Peace on Earth, Goodwill to Men! Perhaps that peace begins immediately after he destroys those repugnant Roman rioters.

To contrast his Beatitudes teachings and his obvious personal serenity with the undeniable conclusion that a tumultuous, pending military engagement is imminent strains my discernment. My mind is ill- prepared to envision a peaceful transition of power. Yet His miracles notwithstanding, I thus conclude raising Lazarus, dead for four days in a tomb, to be concrete evidence of a deity capable of dispatching the legions of Caesar. Our Messiah will triumph.

The Innkeeper's Story

Fulfilling the hostel requirements on any given day is fraught with enough calamity and vendor excuses to compel me to imbibe too much wine, too early in the evening. Compound the routine nuances of being an innkeeper with hosting a festival that the scope of a Passover comprises and the level of frustration and heart rate double. Increase the commercial pressure of accommodating clients with the holy procedure of a seder for the Messiah and you can visualize my consternation.

Innkeepers get bubkes in recognition. But let an embarrassment occur and that disgrace makes him a schmuck. Oy vey!

I am anxious but satisfied that amenities have been addressed. I have hired an additional attendant to manage the desires of those guests' downstairs. I have determined my presence is necessary in the upper room.

CHAPTER SEVENTEEN
A Body Broken

Joseph and I attempt to become inconspicuous in the room as the disciples file in and arrange themselves alongside the Master. We have now assumed the obligation attending to the needs of our guests. The Passover Feast is rife with ritual and one such is the serving of wine four times within the meal. It is not lost on me that Joseph has voluntarily humbled himself to undertake the duties of service to men of a lesser caste. To vicariously partake in this feast with the Messiah is reward enough. We both must continually refocus our thoughts to ensure that all ceremonies are provided.

Suddenly I am overcome with horror. I have neglected to provide a servant for the expected feet washing that precedes the meal. 23. (Luke7:44) I had drawn the water and have the basin nearby but thoughtlessly dismissed the hired servant predictably assigned this task. My mind is racing as I calculate the impact of my lapse in dignity and decorum and fear this offensiveness will cause irreparable damage to my reputation.

And as though my apprehension was sensed by the Master, Jesus walked to my station, smiled at me and retrieved the pitcher and basin only to return to the disciples. He then slips his robe and pours the water into the basin and begins washing and toweling their dirty feet. Each disciple in turn. Each sitting in stunned silence as the Son of Man humbles himself to perform this act of service devoid of any hubris. 24(John 13:14-17)

Upon returning to the feast, I overhear: "You call me Teacher and Lord, and you are right, for so I am. If I then, your Lord and Teacher, have washed your feet, you also ought to wash one another's feet. For I have given you an example, that you also should do just as I have done to you."

All hearts all bursting with the grace we have witnessed. Joseph of Arimathea is literally dancing against the back wall, reciting some liturgy from the Torah I think I recognize as a Psalm King David wrote. My smile is now plastered on my face. Jesus had touched me. He recognized my heart and his knowing smile seem to make me think he had remembered Bina and I that first noel looking into his manger as the child of God. Now this Messiah, sent to free his people and reign as their king, is sharing a Passover in another inn I manage.

The Passover seder meal continues as we watch from our isolated niche. When the hour came, Jesus and his apostles reclined at the table. We listen intently as Jesus admits how eagerly he has anticipated this last supper with his disciples. But I am confused at the statement of how he will suffer and will not eat the Passover meal again until the kingdom of God comes, but my theology is limited. Jesus takes the unleavened bread and the common cup of wine and blesses both remarking, "This is my body given for you; do this in remembrance of me. This cup is the new covenant in my blood, which is poured out for you."

I confess my incomprehension.

There is unsettling talk of betrayal and treachery. Of denial and disputes of greatness among the disciples. Jesus has asked them to follow him to pray outside in the garden, the Mount of Olives. Joseph and I resist the desire to follow them citing their need for privacy. Instead, I begin the mundane task of cleaning the upper room, as any good innkeeper would. Preparing the site for the next occasion. I carefully package the crude, but polished, common cup that was used by Jesus. I opine that this communion ceremony will soon become a perpetual sacrament and how better to observe this ritual in the future than by using the vessel blessed by the Lord.

A few hours later a servant of the chief priest confers with Joseph at the inn. Joseph has been summoned to an emergency meeting of the Jewish council. These seventy-one elders from among the tribes of Israel are ostensibly our governing body excepting for the cruel truth that we Jews are all under the authority of Rome. Joseph reluctantly nods his tacit acceptance of the request and heads off.

It hasn't been lost on me that none of the disciples nor Jesus has returned to the inn. This ominous impression is

The Innkeeper's Story

surpassed by the need for sleep. The combination of hard work and the elation of having Jesus nearby has directed my consciousness into a blissful slumber.

CHAPTER EIGHTEEN
THE CROSS

Whatever bliss attended my sleep was rudely detached as I was awakened by the irrational Joseph ranting how the Sanhedrin was petitioning the Roman Governor Pilate to execute Jesus. Even now the majority of the Council was rallying their allies to support their accusations of blasphemy and insurrection.

His hysteria seems a mixture of fear and anger. I confess reluctance to entertain a notion that the son of God could be so easily subdued by an earthly mandate. I have born witness to miraculous events. I am not convinced there is a need for panic. Didn't our God create the world? Promise the Messiah? Give us Jesus!!

The two of us headed for the Temple and quickly became integrated into a throng of derisive madness. Roman troops and Jewish insurrectionists were shouting nonsense. Our own priests were shouting, "We have no king but Caesar!" The world had gone senseless.

Rounding a Temple corner, I confronted abject horror. Jesus, the Messiah, was being whipped and spat upon by

The Innkeeper's Story

Roman soldiers and a large Jewish crowd was condoning the bloodshed. Only a few citizens among them wept in disbelief and cried for mercy in his behalf. I tore my garment and then fell to my knees. My grief and anger manifest thusly.

A crude wooden cross was presented to Jesus. He was barely able to stand much less walk and the additional weight of that cross defied logic in how he was to manage it out of the courtyard. I screamed profanities at the rebels and was backhanded by a sneering palace guard for my vulgarity. I staggered and dropped down to the stony plaza and tasted blood. What was happening?

How could yesterday's joyous supper be transformed into this tragedy?

Hands reached under my arms and raise this old man to my feet. Joseph was gently lifting me. Tears of disbelief were evident upon his face too as we stared at this unruly mob cheering whenever my Jesus slipped under the bulk of that cross.

Joseph was speaking to me and yet my mind couldn't translate the meaning of his words. This nightmarish scene was scrambling my thoughts as though I was in some drunken stupor. He placed his forehead against mine and slowly repeated his direction and waited for me to look up and acknowledge my understanding with an implicit nod.

I ambled back to the inn with a grotesque purpose before me. My body shivered with anxiety as each step implied the reality of the current situation. Jesus was being crucified today. The serenity of that last supper now being

The Innkeeper's Story

ruined by the discordance of noises associated with this unholy procession.

Joseph of Arimathea had specified a task for me. I was to find Seth and ensure that he would bring his mule and a litter to Golgotha. This hill outside the city gates was often used as a vantage point for all Jewish rebels to witness the merciless murder of other mutineers. Today an innocent was being brutalized on a rugged cross. I would learn later that the stimulus for this crucifixion was directly attributed to our own chief priest and council and not the godless Romans.

At the inn I quickly dispatched three employees to locate Seth and insisted to them how imperative it was for him to come at once. I sat down and buried my head in my hands weeping. I felt so alone. Struggling to find the strength to beckon a young lad, I handed him a coin and instructed him to race back to Bethlehem. He was to relay a message to my wife Bina. "Come quickly to Jerusalem! I need you!"

An incredulous Seth suddenly appears with the servant I had sent. He has heard the news that our Jesus is being tortured and has rounded up several of his followers who are willing to attack the Centurions. I have apparently interrupted his recruitment with the demand he come to me now. His zeal to defend Jesus has now been tempered with the reality that Jesus is near death even as we conspire to protect him. Seth drops his shepherd's staff which was also to be used as his weapon of choice to free Jesus. He too cries shamelessly.

CHAPTER NINETEEN
To The Tomb

I reveal the supremely important role he is to play next. It has fallen to him to provide a virtuous delivery of Jesus' body to a burial site. It shall be his honor to secure our Master's broken body from the cross and protectively escort Jesus to a tomb. Such a task is not without jeopardy and hazard should be expected. Analogous to a shepherd tending a flock among the wild beasts.

His immediate acceptance of this commission was to be expected. He loved Jesus. The very colt that Jesus recently rode triumphantly into Jerusalem upon is nearby, and he is certain that an adequate attachment can be constructed to permit his body to be prudently piloted to the nearby tomb. He hurried away resigned to meet us again by the cross even as the very ground beneath our feet tremored.

Ominous gathering clouds are shielding the sun. There is a sense of foreboding as I begin the arduous journey toward Golgotha, recollecting the epic moments I have experienced with my Jesus. This unremarkable innkeeper has witnessed the glories of God Almighty. So how is it that

The Innkeeper's Story

the King of Kings can be subdued by mere men? Celestial beings had told Seth and other shepherds that first noel that this was our savior. I am at a loss to explain the inconsistencies that perplex me. I must seek the council of learned men.

As I travel up that craggy path, I notice the looks of those backtracking from the knoll. Only hours ago, those very faces were sneering and twisted with scorn for my lord, and now they appear anxious and wary as a child's might if having been caught in a glaring misdeed. It's as though they suddenly are distancing themselves from the transgression that they endorsed this very morning while cheering the decision to recognize sanctimonious piety over indisputable purity. Their contemptuous shouts have become indistinguishable murmurs as they leave this place of skulls, barely raising their heads for fear of being identified as agents sanctioning the murder of the Son of God. Indeed, shouts of cruelty have been replaced with sobs of anguish.

At the top of the knoll are mourners and a squad of Roman soldiers ostensibly there to exact the full measure of life from the trio of men tactlessly being crucified. Some soldiers are gambling for possessions, some are nervously monitoring the skyline as the mounting darkness defies the day's characteristic sun. I spot Jesus' mother among the crowd and can't help but compare her elated appearance as a young mother in our inn's stable birthing her blessed son,

The Innkeeper's Story

to this the older and now heartbroken mother compelled to witness his untimely and cruel death.

The quaking ground beneath our feet and the ominous, darkening sky must be signaling the growing anger of God Almighty. 25.(Matthew 27:51) No one on this hill believes this abnormal physical manifestation is random. Everyone is certain that there will be reckoning not unlike the cities of Sodom and Gomorrah when God dispatched His wrath obliterating those sinners. How much more destructive will God be in retaliation for mankind murdering His holy son Jesus. The fear is tangible.

I am horrified to witness a Roman soldier piercing Jesus' side in an effort to confirm his demise. A hand is unexpectedly placed on my shoulder and as I slowly turn, I am comforted that Joseph of Arimathea 26.(Matthew 27: 57-60) is there. Tears have filled our eyes and we begin blatantly sobbing in grief.

Joseph has approached the soldiers and now hands them a document quickly scanned by the centurion. The soldier nods and signals his men to take Jesus down from his cross. Unpredictably these soldiers appear to possess a genuine regard for the body and are tactful in removing the spikes they once gleefully pounded into his flesh only hours ago. The sign they had mockingly displayed above His head was detached and abruptly discarded in the nearby undergrowth. The sign reflected his accusation: THIS IS JESUS, THE KING OF THE JEWS. 27.(Matthew 27: 37)

The Innkeeper's Story

Seth has now reached us with the litter he hastily designed for the colt. I covertly signal to Seth and motion toward that sign. A statement intended to mock our Lord was now juxtaposed to all disciples as a declaration of truth. Seth casually retrieves it and places it on the litter ostensibly to reinforce the crude assembly that must now bear the weight of Jesus.

Jesus' broken body is gently arranged on the litter to ensure stability as we navigate the rocky and irregular path to the tomb. A shroud of linen blankets shields his offended body.

This tomb was to have been Joseph's final resting place but has now been dedicated as the sepulcher for Jesus. A spontaneous procession of mourners, followers of Jesus, a feeble innkeeper, a member of the Council, and Roman soldiers accompany Seth and his colt as they negotiate the brutal elements of nature to deliver the body of Jesus to the nearby crypt.

Joseph is now accompanied by Nicodemus, a Pharisee and a member of the Jewish council. This Pharisee has anticipated the need to have spices and linens to comply with Jewish burial customs and they gently and ceremoniously attend to this ritual for Jesus within the tomb. A shelf inside the tomb serves as the resting place for the body. 28.(John 19:38-42)

The impending Sabbath hastened the necessity of hurriedly completing the ritual and sealing the cave entrance with a big stone. Though I was of little assistance in moving

The Innkeeper's Story

the rock I felt a compulsion to participate. Seth positioned himself next to me to insure I didn't over exert. He respectfully smiled, even through his grief, in recognition of my attempt.

What treachery had been made manifest! How could a triumphant, heroic entrance into Jerusalem a mere week ago deviate into this most cruel and repulsive crucifixion! Was the Messiah, the anointed one of God, the baby heralded by the angels as the Savior of mankind now dead? Incomprehensible. My mind could not accept what my eyes have viewed.

Seth has noticed my physical reeling and incoherent mumbling and moved to assist me onto the litter, so recently used to transport Jesus, that his blood is still a tacky substance. I am being transported back to the inn atop the sign that only reinforces my astonishment. THIS IS JESUS, THE KING OF THE JEWS.

How could my king, yea, the Son of God, be dead!

CHAPTER TWENTY
THE INN

Bina was pacing and frantic as we approached the Jerusalem inn even as darkness grew into a deeper shade. She had received word too late to attempt the trek up to Golgotha and prudently opted to remain at the Jerusalem inn knowing I would return at some point. The events of the day needing my clarification for her comprehension. As if I am judicious and shrewd enough to distinguish why our kinsmen have abetted in the killing of our Lord. I only give her details without discernment. I am inadequate to analyze the motives and the malice that have taken the life of the King.

My admiration and awe of Jerusalem has been reformed as I cannot separate the holiest of our cities as now being the origin of a conspiracy and betrayal of all precepts associated with the divine. I intend to vacate the city with haste and return to our modest commercial effort in Bethlehem. To live out my remaining days with fond memories linked to my Jesus, my Master.

The Innkeeper's Story

Anon Bina and I ignore the mandate associated with Jewish law to avoid traveling on the Sabbath and we join with other travelers, most of them heathens, in a convoy of varying societies returning to places of commerce, residence, or intrigue. Our destination encompassing the first two. We are propelled by our distain for the piety in Jerusalem coupled with the malevolence they imposed upon Jesus.

Our aged bodies contradict our determination for speed. The pace is slow. Crowded conditions along the dusty road to Bethlehem create the need to shield your face from the sandy residue raised by the shuffling feet of wayfarers. My wheezing suggests frequent stops. My sour disposition is revealed by hurling insults at others just because they are unfortunate enough to be within earshot. I've been done no personal wrong. I'm just angry.

Seth had requested to take us and I summarily dismissed his offer mostly out of deference to my desire to summon a strength any egotistical man might who wants to deny the need of crutches or pity. In retrospect I must admit to a hubris that now threatens to find me decaying by this roadside.

At least I was perceptive enough to have seen the urgency in preserving the now historical and holy sign, taken from the cross. I had also requested Seth to cautiously deviate back to the Jerusalem inn. I gave him directions to the communion cup I had concealed there. He was then to take those infamous nomadic trails and deliver the

The Innkeeper's Story

sanctified vestiges, the cup and emblem, to a safe place among his fellow Bedouins.

I was confident that these were symbolic of a martyred divinity.

Bina and I arrived at our inn shortly before darkness blanketed the countryside. Unusual brilliance was produced by the canopy of stars observable from our vantage point behind the inn. Bina suggested we might want to relocate to the very stable where we witnessed another night where stars emitted a holy light and angels had proclaimed a holy birth and pray there. We clutched one another as we cautiously navigated the uneven stones to the sacred stable and stood there in reverence.

A sudden panic and a jolting pain impaled my chest as I lurched and fell face down onto the stable's soft straw strewn there for the livestock. Uneasy breaths were issued from my lungs and a numbness prevented me from regaining a posture. The frightening realization that Bina was frenetically reacting to my condition was adding to my angst. I didn't want her too ever be so scared. She was inconsolable and her hysterical screams for assistance echoed off the cave walls. Her shrieks produced wide-eyed friends and concerned boarders to my aid. As my mental faculties and respiration slowly returned, they deemed it important to move me back to the inn. For some imperceptible reason I declined that suggestion with a more observable shake of my head. Bina concurred that the more manageable setting for doctors and necessities was here, in the stable for now.

She issued orders for blankets, available medicines and even our stuffed mattress be relocated to the stable. Tomorrow she would assess the need to reevaluate moving back to the inn. Therapeutically, the obvious requirement was rest and peace. The few livestock inside the cave were ushered to the grove.

My labored breathing was returning to a more normal rhythm and the paralysis lessened, leaving only an immobility in my left arm to remind me of my outwardly dire emergency. I fell into a slumber filled with memories of my life. Regrets that should have never occurred haunted my thoughts. Unkind words I'd spoken, apathy I'd expressed to those in need, failures of compassion toward my fellow man and sins for pettiness of devoutness. I silently prayed for forgiveness even in my unconsciousness. Upon awakening I experienced a sense of unprecedented peacefulness. I was happy, even joyous, and greeted visitors with a warmth and beauty heretofore an unknown characteristic of this old innkeeper.

And even though I was perhaps able to return to my bedroom inside the inn, I had implored Bina to let me remain with the animals in this section of the stable now decorated with my necessities. She had reluctantly agreed noting that it appeared to cheer me, and my recovery was improving beyond expectations.

CHAPTER TWENTY-ONE
HE LIVES

It has been a week since our Lord was horribly crucified and buried in that tomb. News that His resurrection occurred has reached our inn and conspiracy theories flourish.

Roman soldiers that guarded his tomb supposedly had been awestruck by an unearthly apparition that appeared and rolled away the stone. They grudgingly admitted to being too frozen in fear to move and unable to intervene. But rumors soon surfaced of those same guards accepting an inducement from the priests suggesting instead that Jesus' disciples had repossessed the body and no angels were ever present. 29.(Matthew 28:12-15)

Jewish leaders have contrived the theory that zealous disciples paid off the Romans and removed the body to complete the charade that he would die and be raised again in three days. But followers of Jesus have confirmed his resurrection attesting to his visits with them. Even reputable women have established their encounter with the risen King and noted his visage capable of eating and drinking. There is elation among his followers and distress amid those responsible for this travesty.

My heart rejoices as I now am convinced that my Jesus is alive. My faith has been restored much like the faith of the disciples who also could not comprehend the love we all witnessed. The words of mercy and acts of miracles performed should have been enough for us. But we were all too weak. Now there is nothing we cannot overcome in His name – even death.

Seth has come to visit. Bina has prepared a glorious meal and although loath to serve it here in the stable, she has approved it on the condition this is my last night to reside here.

The lamb meat Seth has provided is such a delicacy. And Bina has never looked more beautiful even as she barks orders for how we mustn't eat like the pigs of the Gentiles. Her food is delicious. We all laugh. We have hope again. Jesus lives.

Seth's white colt is nearby and from the saddlebag he fetches his shepherd's drum and begins the rhythmic cadence. Everyone's mind fondly recalls that noel when as a younger boy he provided this gift of music to the newly-born son of God.

Bina and I were holding hands when the jolt in my chest overwhelmed me. The astonished expression on her face was my last image of humanity as my eyes closed and my hand slipped from her grasp.

The Innkeeper's Story

Only the merest of moments elapsed before the inexplicable. Standing in front of me was my Jesus. My Lord! My God! His outstretched hand, inclusive of an offensive nail scar, was reaching for my hand. A supremacy from his radiant smile and perceptive gaze, as he scanned the stable, seemed to lift me to my feet although this form was no longer wracked with pain. It too was a resurrected body.

The expression on my now lifeless body was one of peace and comfort. Bina paused to more closely examine my feature. Seth stopped drumming but only to shout his alleluia. And though tears seeped from his eyes his praise for my deliverance unto an eternity with God reached a crescendo that surely woke our inn' guests as it reverberated off the limestone.

This is the Innkeeper's Story...

SCRIPTURAL REFERENCES

(6) Exodus 30: 11-16 1 Then the Lord said to Moses, 12 "When you take a census of the Israelites to count them, each one must pay the Lord a ransom for his life at the time he is counted. Then no plague will come on them when you number them. 13 Each one who crosses over to those already counted is to give a half shekel,[a] according to the sanctuary shekel, which weighs twenty gerahs. This half shekel is an offering to the Lord. 14 All who cross over, those twenty years old or more, are to give an offering to the Lord. 15 The rich are not to give more than a half shekel and the poor are not to give less when you make the offering to the Lord to atone for your lives. 16 Receive the atonement money from the Israelites and use it for the service of the tent of meeting. It will be a memorial for the Israelites before the Lord, making atonement for your lives."

(1) Numbers 15: 37-41 37 And the LORD spake unto Moses, saying, 38 Speak unto the children of Israel, and bid them that they make them fringes in the borders of their garments throughout their generations, and that they put upon the fringe of the borders a ribband of blue: 39 And it shall be unto you for a fringe, that ye may look upon it, and remember all the commandments of

The Innkeeper's Story

the LORD, and do them; and that ye seek not after your own heart and your own eyes, after which ye use to go a whoring:40 That ye may remember, and do all my commandments, and be holy unto your God.41 I am the LORD your God, which brought you out of the land of Egypt, to be your God: I am the LORD your God.

(19) Judges 5:10 Tell of it, ye that ride on white asses, Ye that sit on rich carpets, And ye that walk by the way. Far from the noise of archers, in the places of drawing water, There shall they rehearse the righteous acts of Jehovah, Even the righteous acts of his rule in Israel. Then the people of Jehovah went down to the gates."

(2) 2Kings 17:27-33) 27 Then the king of Assyria gave this order: "Have one of the priests you took captive from Samaria go back to live there and teach the people what the god of the land requires." 28 So one of the priests who had been exiled from Samaria came to live in Bethel and taught them how to worship the Lord. 29 Nevertheless, each national group made its own gods in the several towns where they settled, and set them up in the shrines the people of Samaria had made at the high places. 30 The people from Babylon made Sukkoth Benoth, those from Kuthah made Nergal, and those from Hamath made Ashima; 31 the Avvites made Nibhaz and Tartak, and the Sepharvites burned their children in the fire as sacrifices to Adrammelek and Anammelek, the gods of Sepharvaim. 32 They worshiped the Lord, but they also appointed all sorts of their own people to officiate for them as priests in the shrines at the high places. 33 They worshiped the

Lord, but they also served their own gods in accordance with the customs of the nations from which they had been brought.

(4) 1Samuel 16:1 16 The Lord said to Samuel, "How long will you mourn for Saul, since I have rejected him as king over Israel? Fill your horn with oil and be on your way; I am sending you to Jesse of Bethlehem. I have chosen one of his sons to be king."

(10) 1Samuel 16:11-12 11 So he asked Jesse, "Are these all the sons you have? " "There is still the youngest," Jesse answered. "He is tending the sheep." Samuel said, "Send for him; we will not sit down until he arrives."12 So he sent for him and had him brought in. He was glowing with health and had a fine appearance and handsome features. Then the Lord said, "Rise and anoint him; this is the one."

(11) Matthew 2: 9-12 After they had heard the king, they went on their way, and the star they had seen when it rose went ahead of them until it stopped over the place where the child was. 10 When they saw the star, they were overjoyed. 11 On coming to the house, they saw the child with his mother Mary, and they bowed down and worshiped him. Then they opened their treasures and presented him with gifts of gold, frankincense and myrrh. 12 And having been warned in a dream not to go back to Herod, they returned to their country by another route.

The Innkeeper's Story

(12) Matthew 2:16-17 16 When Herod realized that he had been outwitted by the Magi, he was furious, and he gave orders to kill all the boys in Bethlehem and its vicinity who were two years old and under, in accordance with the time he had learned from the Magi. 17 Then what was said through the prophet Jeremiah was fulfilled:

(14) Matthew 3: 4-7 4 John's clothes were made of camel's hair, and he had a leather belt around his waist. His food was locusts and wild honey. 5 People went out to him from Jerusalem and all Judea and the whole region of the Jordan. 6 Confessing their sins, they were baptized by him in the Jordan River.

(15) Matthew 3:16 16 As soon as Jesus was baptized, he went up out of the water. At that moment heaven was opened, and he saw the Spirit of God descending like a dove and alighting on him. 17 And a voice from heaven said, "This is my Son, whom I love; with him I am well pleased."

(27) Matthew 27:37 37 Above his head they placed the written charge against him: this is jesus, the king of the jews.

(25) Matthew 27:51 At that moment the curtain of the temple was torn in two from top to bottom. The earth shook, the rocks split 52 and the tombs broke open.

(26) Matthew: 27: 57-60 As evening approached, there came a rich man from Arimathea, named Joseph, who had himself become a disciple of Jesus. 58 Going to Pilate, he asked for Jesus' body, and Pilate ordered that

it be given to him. 59 Joseph took the body, wrapped it in a clean linen cloth, 60 and placed it in his own new tomb that he had cut out of the rock. He rolled a big stone in front of the entrance to the tomb and went away.

(29) Matthew 28:12-15 12 When the chief priests had met with the elders and devised a plan, they gave the soldiers a large sum of money, 13 telling them, "You are to say, 'His disciples came during the night and stole him away while we were asleep.' 14 If this report gets to the governor, we will satisfy him and keep you out of trouble." 15 So the soldiers took the money and did as they were instructed. And this story has been widely circulated among the Jews to this very day.

(20) Mark 11:1-6) And when they draw-near to Jerusalem—to Bethphage and Bethany, near the Mount of Olives—He sends-forth two of His disciples, 2 and says to them, "Go to the village before you. And immediately while proceeding into it, you will find a colt having been tied, on which none of mankind[a] yet sat. Untie it, and be bringing it. 3 And if someone says to you, 'Why are you doing this?', say, 'The Lord has need of it, and[b] immediately He sends[c] it back here[d]'". 4 And they went and found a colt having been tied at a door, outside on the street. And they untie it. 5 And some of the ones standing there were saying to them, "What are you doing untying the colt?" 6 But the ones spoke to them just as Jesus spoke, and they permitted them. And they bring the colt to Jesus.

The Innkeeper's Story

(7) Luke 1: 8-10 8 Once when Zechariah's division was on duty and he was serving as priest before God, 9 he was chosen by lot, according to the custom of the priesthood, to go into the temple of the Lord and burn incense. 10 And when the time for the burning of incense came, all the assembled worshipers were praying outside.

(8) Luke 1: 18-22 18 Zechariah asked the angel, "How can I be sure of this? I am an old man and my wife is well along in years." 19 The angel said to him, "I am Gabriel. I stand in the presence of God, and I have been sent to speak to you and to tell you this good news. 20 And now you will be silent and not able to speak until the day this happens, because you did not believe my words, which will come true at their appointed time." 21 Meanwhile, the people were waiting for Zechariah and wondering why he stayed so long in the temple. 22 When he came out, he could not speak to them. They realized he had seen a vision in the temple, for he kept making signs to them but remained unable to speak.

(9) Luke 1:62-79 62 Then they made signs to his father, to find out what he would like to name the child. 63 He asked for a writing tablet, and to everyone's astonishment he wrote, "His name is John." 64 Immediately his mouth was opened and his tongue set free, and he began to speak, praising God. 65 All the neighbors were filled with awe, and throughout the hill country

The Innkeeper's Story

of Judea people were talking about all these things. 66 Everyone who heard this wondered about it, asking, "What then is this child going to be?" For the Lord's hand was with him.

(5) Luke 2:1-4 In those days Caesar Augustus issued a decree that a census should be taken of the entire Roman world. 2 (This was the first census that took place while[a] Quirinius was governor of Syria.) 3 And everyone went to their own town to register.4 So Joseph also went up from the town of Nazareth in Galilee to Judea, to Bethlehem the town of David, because he belonged to the house and line of David.

(13) Luke 2: 41-50 41 Every year Jesus' parents went to Jerusalem for the Festival of the Passover. 42 When he was twelve years old, they went up to the festival, according to the custom. 43 After the festival was over, while his parents were returning home, the boy Jesus stayed behind in Jerusalem, but they were unaware of it. 44 Thinking he was in their company, they traveled on for a day. Then they began looking for him among their relatives and friends. 45 When they did not find him, they went back to Jerusalem to look for him. 46 After three days they found him in the temple courts, sitting among the teachers, listening to them and asking them questions. 47 Everyone who heard him was amazed at his understanding and his answers. 48 When his parents saw him, they were astonished. His mother said to him, "Son, why have you treated us like this? Your father and I have been anxiously searching for you."49 "Why were you searching for me?" he asked. "Didn't

The Innkeeper's Story

you know I had to be in my Father's house?"[a] 50 But they did not understand what he was saying to them.

(16) Luke 4: 18-20; 28 "The Spirit of the Lord is on me, because he has anointed me to proclaim good news to the poor. He has sent me to proclaim freedom for the prisoners and recovery of sight for the blind, to set the oppressed free, to proclaim the year of the Lord's favor."[20 Then he rolled up the scroll, gave it back to the attendant and sat down. The eyes of everyone in the synagogue were fastened on him. 28 All the people in the synagogue were furious when they heard this.

(23) Luke 7:44 Then he turned toward the woman and said to Simon, "Do you see this woman? I came into your house. You did not give me any water for my feet, but she wet my feet with her tears and wiped them with her hair.

(3) (17) Luke 10: 30-35 30 In reply Jesus said: "A man was going down from Jerusalem to Jericho, when he was attacked by robbers. They stripped him of his clothes, beat him and went away, leaving him half dead. 31 A priest happened to be going down the same road, and when he saw the man, he passed by on the other side. 32 So too, a Levite, when he came to the place and saw him, passed by on the other side. 33 But a Samaritan, as he traveled, came where the man was; and when he saw him, he took pity on him. 34 He went to him and bandaged his wounds, pouring on oil and wine. Then he put the man on his own donkey, brought him to an inn and took care of him. 35 The next day he took out two denarii[e] and gave them to the innkeeper. 'Look

after him,' he said, 'and when I return, I will reimburse you for any extra expense you may have.

(21) Luke 22:10 He replied, "As you enter the city, a man carrying a jar of water will meet you. Follow him to the house that he enters,

(22) Luke 22: 11-12 Then you shall say to the master of the house, 'The Teacher says to you, "Where is the guest room where I may eat the Passover with My disciples?" ' Then he will show you a large, furnished upper room; there make ready.

(18) John11: 43-45 43 When he had said this, Jesus called in a loud voice, "Lazarus, come out!" 44 The dead man came out, his hands and feet wrapped with strips of linen, and a cloth around his face. Jesus said to them, "Take off the grave clothes and let him go."

(24) John 13: 14-17 13 "You call me 'Teacher' and 'Lord,' and rightly so, for that is what I am. 14 Now that I, your Lord and Teacher, have washed your feet, you also should wash one another's feet. 15 I have set you an example that you should do as I have done for you. 16 Very truly I tell you, no servant is greater than his master, nor is a messenger greater than the one who sent him. 17 Now that you know these things, you will be blessed if you do them.

(28) John 19:38-42) 38 Later, Joseph of Arimathea asked Pilate for the body of Jesus. Now Joseph was a disciple of Jesus, but secretly because he feared the Jewish leaders. With Pilate's permission, he came and took the body away. 39 He was accompanied by Nicodemus, the

The Innkeeper's Story

man who earlier had visited Jesus at night. Nicodemus brought a mixture of myrrh and aloes, about seventy-five pounds.[e] 40 Taking Jesus' body, the two of them wrapped it, with the spices, in strips of linen. This was in accordance with Jewish burial customs. 41 At the place where Jesus was crucified, there was a garden, and in the garden a new tomb, in which no one had ever been laid. 42 Because it was the Jewish day of Preparation and since the tomb was nearby, they laid Jesus there.

Printed in the USA
CPSIA information can be obtained
at www.ICGtesting.com
LVHW021515121123
763715LV00046B/885